DICTIO

C0-APN-063

Compiled and Edited by

AMY BROWN

JOHN DOWNING

JOHN SCEATS

JOVE BOOKS, NEW YORK

PRIMARY DICTIONARY SERIES: DICTIONARY 1

A Jove Book / published by arrangement with
W. & R. Chambers, Ltd.

PRINTING HISTORY
Six previous printings
W. & R. Chambers edition published 1971
Jove edition / February 1979

ISBN: 0-515-09093-X

Library of Congress Catalog Card Number: 71-152246

Jove Books are published by The Berkley Publishing Group,
200 Madison Avenue, New York, New York 10016.
The name "JOVE" and the "J" logo
are trademarks belonging to Jove Publications, Inc.

PRINTED IN THE UNITED STATES OF AMERICA

20   19   18   17   16   15   14   13   12   11

acorns

airport

ambulance

anchor

apple

apron

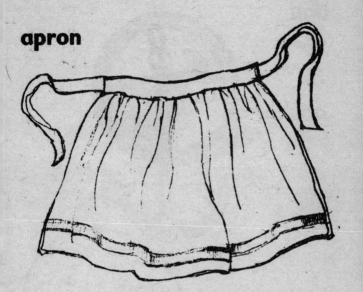

arrow

ball

balloons

banana

basket

b **B**

bed

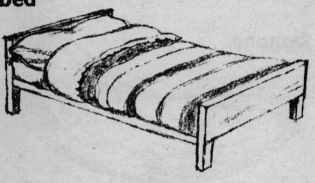

bee

birds

boat

book

bread

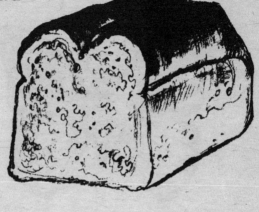

bridge

butterfly

button

camel

candle

car

carrot

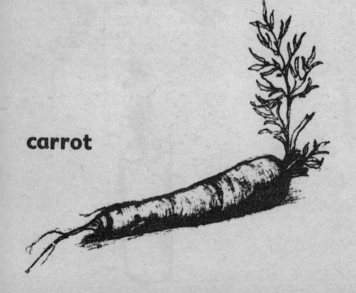

castle

cat

chair

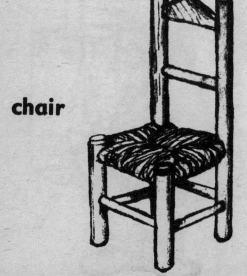

clock

clown

cobweb

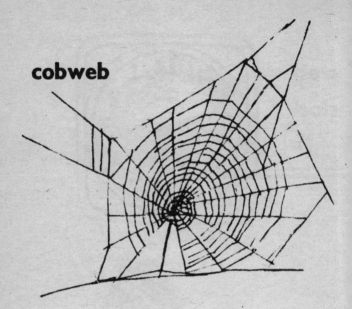

cow

crab

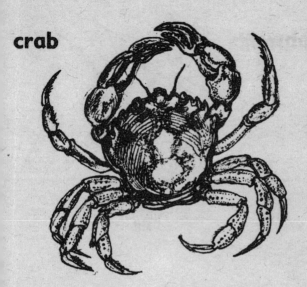

cup

daffodil

daisy

d **D**

deer

dog

d **D**

doll

donkey

door

dragon

drum

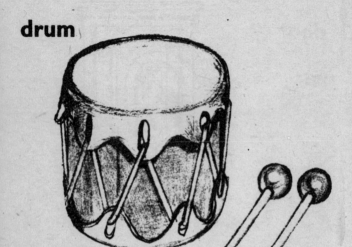

duck

ear

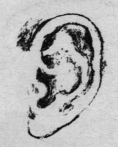

egg

elephant

envelope

eye

fairy

farm

feather

fence

fire engine

fish

flowers

fork

fountain

fox

frog

g   G

gate

g   **G**

giraffe

glasses

glove

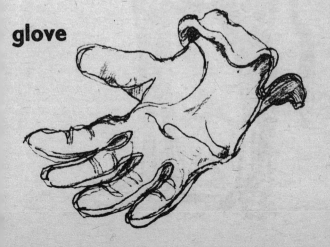

goat

goldfish

g　　　　　　　　　　　　G

guitar

h   H

hammer

hand

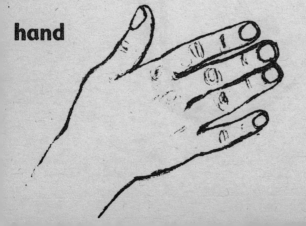

h H

helicopter

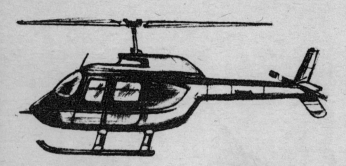

hen

h   H

horse

h H

house

ice cream

icicles

iron

j   J

jug

k   **K**

kangaroo

kettle

k   **K**

keys

king

k   K

kite

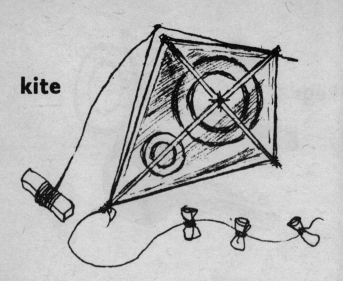

kitten

ladder

lamb

leaf

lemon

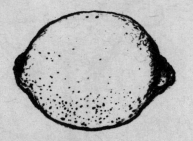

lion

monkey

moon

mountain

mouse

necklace

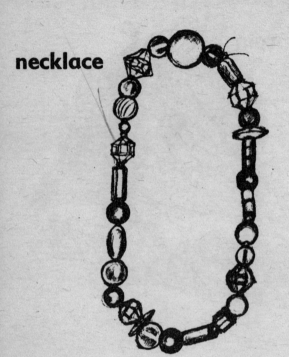

needle

nest

nose

o   O

orange

owl

parachute

parrot

pear

pencil

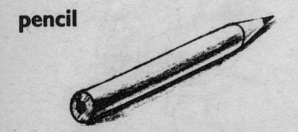

pig

pigeon

pony

puppy

q   9

queen

rabbit

rainbow

reindeer

ring

r

R

river

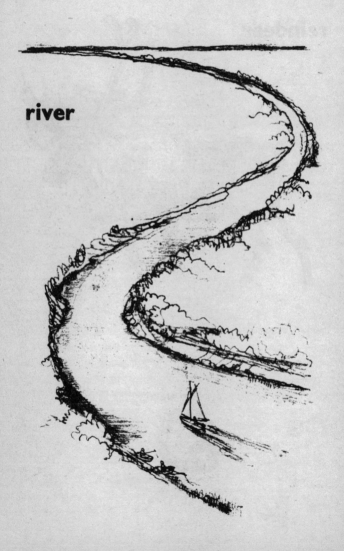

rocket

roof

rope

rose

sandwich

saw

scissors

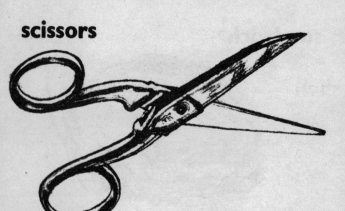

sheep

shell

shoes

snail

snake

snowman

spider

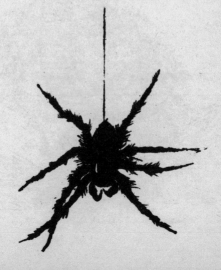

spoon

squirrel

star

stool

sun

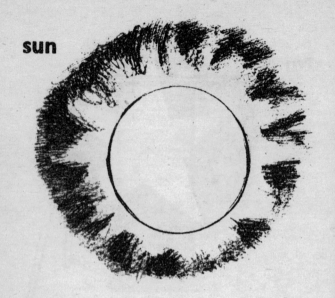

swan

swing

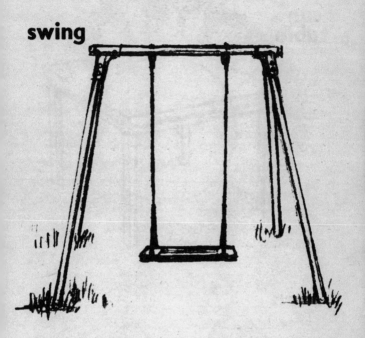

sword

table

telephone

television

tent

tiger

tractor

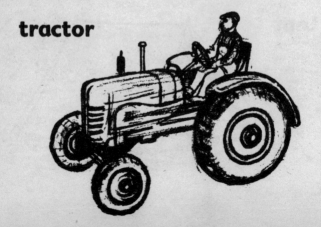

t   T

train

tree

trumpet

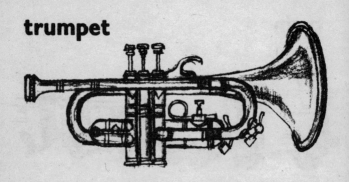

tulip

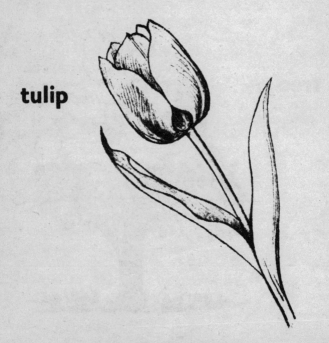

umbrella

van

vase

wall

watch

whale

wheel

whistle

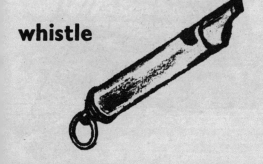

wigwam

windmill

window

witch

wolf

xylophone

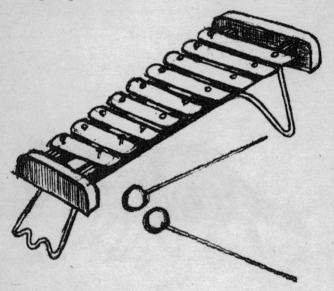

y   Y

yo-yo

zebra